ISN: 979-8-218-76964-2
First Edition: November, 2025

For permissions, contact:

[Purposefully Jasrial]
[jasrial.com]

CONTENTS

ACKNOWLEDGEMENTS

This book is dedicated to those who are navigating their path in this world. May you find strength and solace as you open yourself to new perspectives and begin to transform your reality. You are never alone, for God is always walking with you. Take a moment listen to the quiet wisdom within and embrace the lessons that come with growth.

All glory and honor to the Most High God, who planted this message within me, and sustained me through every season. The purpose of this book is to call us all deeper into truth, alignment, and healing.

To my family; Thank you for your love, support, and presence. Your impact shaped the foundation this message originated from. Thank you for holding space for who I was and who I'm becoming.

To my friends and community; I am grateful your encouragement, honesty, and prayers. Your presence has been proof that God can speaks through anyone.

To the reader; I hope these pages encourage you. Your path is still unfolding, full of promises as you remember the Promiser walks with you.

With love & reverence,

Jasrial

THE BEGINNING

1 The beginning of time is irrelevant until you cultivate your time here on Earth with purpose. Every soul is born into this world with a divine assignment. To make an impact, transform perception, help one another walk in truth and righteousness. There was silence and stillness before there was any creation on Earth. There was no fear, for fear hadn't yet been conceived. There was no sorrow, for grief had never whispered a name. All the things we experience: worry, fear, anxiety, stress, doubt, e.g. did not exist in the beginning. The first breath into the world came from stillness. *The breathe of life.* It carried the Spirit of Light, unseen by humans eyes, for the eyes had not yet opened. God created all we see today through eternal flame, unexplainable love, divine consciousness, and scatter it across the entire Earth. God desire has always been for us to experience perfect peace, radiant love, and a deep knowing that surpasses human understanding.

"For my thoughts are not your thoughts, neither are your ways My ways," said the Lord. For as the heavens are higher than the earth, so are My ways higher than your ways, and My thoughts than your thoughts." - Isaiah 55:5-9.

The beauty of life lies in uncertainty. To trust God is letting go of needing to know how everything will unfold. When we align our will with faith. We begin to walk in the promises that have always been ours, which is unshakable, sacred, and eternal. Promises that are given onto us are set in stone, forever flowing to those who walk in righteousness. When God brings your mind from a state of unawareness to awareness, there is a separation. Fear is not an enemy, but a teacher. Worry emerged not as a curse, but as a signal. Whenever we begin to think, instead of being present. It causes reactions instead of reflections. It causes towers and walls to be built instead of sacred teachings God places in your heart though the spirit.

The Most High will not leave you, nor forsake you. Everything you go through, every trial, setback, or delay is meant to awaken you. When the power of God rises within you, not by force but by revelation. Your mind returns to its true function: a vessel, not the master. The heart will speak, and the mind will listen. Peace will no longer be an external wish, but will be who you are. Those who walk with God shall not live in confusion, nor fear the darkness. We shall think with clarity. We shall love with purity. We shall dwell in peace, as in the beginning. Our bodies are flesh. We have two minds, the mind of the world and the mind of the Spirit. The mind of the Spirit communes with God, seeks wisdom, lives in peace, and reflects the glory of God. Confusion does not come from God. God is not the author of chaos, but of righteousness.

Life lessons are meant to learn, so you can always evolve into your highest potential. It's never appropriate to assume someone "chose" their trauma, but the truth is that God can transform that pain into purpose. The balance of light and darkness keeps us evaluating: *Am I growing? Or am I indulging?* Regardless of what you have experienced, your past is not your prison. It is your testimony. God values the inner beauty of the quiet strength, the resilience, the truth which outshines outward adornment. Your soul already knew what it could overcome before you entered this life. God had that much faith in you. You were already set apart, appointed and gloriously made.

As an adult; you choose which attributes, values, morals, and identity you carry forward. When you come to the realization of free will, the awareness brings transformation. When you become an adult, you take ownership and power over your life. You are the example now for your children, your nieces, nephews, friends, family, partner and even strangers. When the Spirit of Truth comes, it will guide you into All Truth.

Everyone at some point of time has dealt with life or dealing with life as we continue on through this journey. Everyone is seeking and searching for genuine pure love with no guidance or direction on where to start. Everyone is doing their best mentally, spiritually, and emotionally to take care of themselves while supporting others. Those who feel the lowest of lows, uninspired, clouded routine of emotions, experiences, or excuses. Take a moment to ask yourself the following questions:

* *Are you still breathing and supplied with everything you need?*

❖ Have you asked God for peace of mind? For clarity? For strength?

❖ Are you choosing to shrink? Or are you ready to rise and reclaim who God has called you to be?

Be loving towards yourself. Love is patient, kind, unconditional, goodness, faithfulness, gentleness, and self control. Let that love begin with you.

THE BLUEPRINT OF YOUR MIND
WILL CHANGE YOUR LIFE

2 To truly understand someone, you must first understand what has shaped them into who they are. While this book explores vulnerability; it cannot be fully conveyed through black-and-white pages if you never witnessed it firsthand. We must be mindful to not judge others unless we are prepared to be judged ourselves. Be careful not to mistreat others, for one day, you will need grace to be extended to you. The same measure you use will be measured back to you. ***If you had to take a selfie of your outwardly appearance and your spirit, would they align?*** Your inner appearance is reflected in the fruits of the Spirit, which shapes your outward behavior. In the end, your character will speak louder than anything you possess.

Empathy begins with listening, not indulging, not repairing, nor pleasing. It's wise not to become a people pleaser, nor should you strive to be one. Honesty and authenticity should be valued, even when they make others uncomfortable. ***How do you expect God to bless a falsified version of you, instead of the person God created you to be?***

When you start to care more about someone's well-being than their temporary comfort, you begin to make a real impact. We gain a deeper understanding of life by observing the world's constant changes and the pressures we all face. A grateful mind begins to emerge and through that gratitude is awakening. We realize that the purest diamonds are formed under pressure.

Genuine listening helps us become more attentive with not what is said, but to what is *meant*. Everyone should strive to be quick to listen, slow to speak, and slow to anger. Striving to do better while keeping your head high is a blessing. One prayer I often say is: **"God, allow me to humble myself and open my heart to do so."** I prefer to choose humility before life has to teach me the hard way. Recognizing your strengths is important, but it doesn't change the fact we are all human and vulnerable. Stub your toe on a table, it will still hurt. So instead of developing an attitude of invisibility, cultivate a mindset of resilience that walks with humility and compassion.

When I was an athlete, I had the choice to pursue sports in college or focus on academics. I chose to dedicate myself to something I knew would stay with me for life, my mind. Physical abilities can only take you so far, but they can be a bridge to help you to where you want to go. We all have talents, gifts, opportunities, and assignments. However, the gift of *free will* allows you to choose: **Will we be the subject or the entertainment?** If you choose to be the subject, you will lead, create, and live with intention. If you choose to be entertainment, you will perform, distract or exist for others' amusement. One path holds purpose. The other holds performance.

Your mindset will determine how far you will go in life. If you rely too much on others or follow the crowd; you'll never develop you own independent thinking. Instead, your mind will simply mirror those around you. Full of noise, but lacking substance. God gave us one mouth and two ears for a reason; to listen more than we speak. We should listen to our discernment and not lean on our own understanding. Humility reminds us that what goes up must come down. Life itself is filled with valuable lessons on how to live, love, and grow. If you always view yourself as a victim and blame others for your situation. It reflects a denial of your own responsibility and limits your growth.

* *If you claim to love yourself, why are you being dishonest with the truth?*

* *If you truly love yourself, why do you feel the need to impress others instead of simply being who you are?*

To find peace, you must first identify the roots of your insecurity. When your mind is clouded and the weight of the world feels to heavy, pause. Be still! Give thanks for your current existence. ***If you don't like the life you're living, what are you going to do about it?*** Changing your life shouldn't involve self-demoralization, harming others, or using others. It's an internal process of reevaluating your direction, reshaping your perspective, and committing to growth. Many people live in environments they didn't choose, but they still have the power to choose how they live within them. Ask yourself:

* *How are you going to change your life?*

* *What talents or passions can you purse to help you move forward?*

* *What are your gifts? Do you love to speak, host, produce, guide, create, or teach?*

Find people in your life who share your mindset, values, and morals. Build relationships rooted in respect and honesty. Then go and change the world around you, while improving yourself along the way.

Why is generosity so important? Because it recognizes that everyone is carrying silent burdens. While misery loves company, it's difficult to comprehend the malice of those who intentionally hurt others. Life is about transitioning from one place, one mindset, or one season to the next. Strong values and moral convictions are the foundation of a meaningful life. As the saying goes: *If you don't stand for something, you'll settle for anything.*

Emotional intelligence is rare. Children express feelings without filters, but many adults still do the same. This lack of self-awareness leads to conflict, poor communication, and impulsive decisions. When you walk in the peace that God gives, you no longer engage in foolish arguments or conversations. When people become emotionally attached to beliefs that don't bear fruit, it often mirrors a child's tantrum. Stay away from being mislead, because bad company corrupts good character. Ask yourself:

❖ *How do you respond when others act out emotionally?*

❖ *Do you pause and pray for them? Do you argue, or lead by example?*

❖ *Does your reaction resemble the fruits of the Spirit?*

As children, we didn't worry about responsibilities or consequences. We dreamed freely. As adults, we must hold onto that childlike wonder while increasing our wisdom to discern and set boundaries. Wisdom helps us recognize wolves in sheep's clothing. Stay true to yourself, facing each situation with honesty, courage, and peace. Boundaries are divinely essential for others and ourselves. Even God set boundaries in the beginning of time, proving that even freedom has limits. Involving yourself with those whose hearts are filled with darkness will only pull you down. Let God do what the Most High does best. When you are in alignment with the Spirit of God, it marks the end of one season and the beginning of another.

If you still act impulsively, pause and ask why. Discernment and awareness comes from the fruits of the Spirit. It will keep you on the path of righteousness. Mutual respect can bridge the gaps between our different journeys. You walk the path of righteousness when your heart is free of anger, unforgiveness, and bitterness. If you continue to indulge in distractions and let emotions control you, you choose the path of destruction of your soul.

"For we wrestle not against flesh and blood, but against principalities, against powers, against the rulers of the darkness of this world, against spiritual wickedness in high places."

Ephesians 6:12

If you're constantly seeking approval or attention, you'll never know the freedom of being your true self. The childlike essence is the real you, which can get buried under the weight of performance and perfectionism. It's okay to change your mind. It's okay to choose a new path. My advice is to spend some time with God in solitude. Rediscover yourself in the image that God sees you, not what the world tried to make you into. Make sacrifices that align with your purpose. It's a blessing when someone sees the light within you, but it's more powerful when *you* start to see it in yourself. We are meant to help each other along the journey to remind each other who God created us to be. If you know your ego is drawn to darkness, don't let fear of the light keep you from your own healing. Embrace the power God bestowed within you, since the moment you

were born. You are not here to impress the world.
You are here to *redeem*.

GETTING YOUR FEET WET

3 Each new chapter in your life unfolds uniquely, shaping your personal story. Every expected or unexpected experience, prepares you for what is ahead. These moments are opportunities to grow, reflect, and gain wisdom. *Getting Your Feet Wet* means stepping into something unfamiliar for the first time and learning as you go. Starting a new job, moving to a new city, or forming new relationships all require a period of adjustment. You must learn the rhythms, observe the environment, and decide how to show up. It takes time to build good habits, understand culture, and discover what you truly value. Life constantly offers new terrain to explore. Every experience challenges you to grow, adapt, and evolve. Some moments will bring joy, while others may be difficult. But in every season, seek God's guidance to help you walk with wisdom and peace.

* *How do you approach unfamiliar situations?*
* *Do you find new experiences exciting or overwhelming?*
* *Are you adaptable?*

It's important to learn contentment in all seasons. God knows your needs and will strengthen you accordingly. Facing the unknown can either stretch your perspective or limit your growth. Often, the things that feel overwhelming at first is actually an opportunity to grow and mature spiritually. You must surrender: to God, to the moment, and to the unfamiliar. ***How can the Most High show up on your behalf, if you are always in the way?*** If you're easily shaken, pulled out of character, or driven by emotion, you're delaying your own development. Stand firm in faith. Be courageous and alert. Ask yourself:

* *How do you manage new experiences? How do you maneuver through them?*

* *Are you reactive, letting circumstances control your emotions?*

* *Are you proactive, grounded in your values and making intentional choices?*

Authenticity and Growth

Everyone maneuvers, manages, and conducts themselves differently. New experiences can be spiritual, mental, or psychological tests. Meet each new experiences with reflection, adaptability, and resilience. Growth is a lifelong journey that blends your past lessons and future uncertainties. How you respond reveals your character. Everyone has a unique conditioning shaped by environment, upbringing, emotional maturity, and lived experiences. To navigate new terrain, lead with grace and practice intentional self-reflection.

In today's digital age, many feel pressured to perform or pretend. Pretending to be someone you're not often stems from insecurity. Seeking validation through false image separates you from your true self and even from God. It's better to be accepted for who you are than admired for who you pretend to be. That false identity leads to inner conflict and loss of purpose. Many people present fake versions of themselves hoping to gain love, respect or status. But *Romans 12:2* reminds us:

"Do not conform to the patterns of this world, but transformed by renewing of your mind. Then you will be able to test and approve what God's will is-good, pleasing, and perfect will."

Examine how you conduct yourself and how you treat others:

* *Are you genuine? Are you sincere?*

* *Do you give freely, expecting nothing in return? Or do you keep score?*

* *Do you walk in truth? Or uphold a facade to maintain an illusion?*

Growth begins with honest reflection. ***Does that feel uncomfortable for you? Are you afraid of what you'll discover?*** There's a reason it's called **shadow work**. When you take time to look at your past behaviors, beliefs, and reactions. You take a major step toward emotional and spiritual maturity. Self-awareness is the foundation for self-control. **Are you walking in faith? Do you recognize that God is with you?** If not, it may be time to examine the condition of your heart.

Perceive failure not as a final verdict, but as a stepping stone. When disappointment comes, shift your lens: maybe it's not rejection but redirection. *Psalm 5:10* says:

"Create in me a pure heart, O God, and renew a steadfast spirit within me."

A small shift in perception transforms every challenge into an opportunity. Spiritually, this means examining your values and beliefs. You may discover your past is influencing your present more than you realize. As new questions arise, meet them with curiosity and humility. Let your moral compass guide you through unfamiliar waters.

People assume that older generations are set in their ways, but many younger people are equally resistant. Life is meant for all of us to not only learn from each other, but grow as well. When life presents new people, ideas, or environments, adaptability becomes essential. The faster you adapt, the more effectively you can grow and walk in purpose. *Ephesians 4:22-24* says:

"You were taught, with regard to your former way of life, to put off your old self, which is being corrupted by its deceitful desires; to be made new in the attitude of your minds; and to put on the new self, created to be like God in true righteousness and holiness."

Adaptability invites thoughtful response over impulsive reaction. If you're exposed to a new culture, for instance, being flexible helps you release old assumptions and embrace new perspectives. Your norm might be foreign to someone else, too. Flexibility challenges your patterns of thought. Rigid thinking resists change. Everything shifts when you view change as expansion, not a threat to your identity. You begin to see the bigger picture.

Resilience in Faith

Where is your faith? Do you fully understand what faith is? Letting go of limiting beliefs allows *true* faith to flourish. Spiritual growth becomes less about following rigid rules and more about an intimate relationship with God and with yourself. Too many systems are designed to keep people stagnant. God, however, liberates. You have to observe areas in your life where you have limited yourself. Sometimes it feels like you're close to a breakthrough, yet surrounded by silence. When you're taking a test, the teacher is often silent during the exam. Likewise, when God is preparing you for your purpose, it may feel like silence. It's not a test of temptation. It's a test of faithfulness, obedience, and endurance within your spirit. ***Would you rather grow gently under God's guidance or be pushed by the world?***

Resilience is the trait that separates those who thrive from those who fold. Not every season is joyful. You'll face loss, hardship, and disappointment. But how you respond shows your character. Emotionally mature people handle fear, anxiety, and doubt without letting those emotions rule them. Emotions signify that we are alive. Emotional discipline helps ensure they don't lead your life. A lack of emotional control often reveals a lack of self-discipline. If you aspire to be resilient, here's the truth: *Resilient people see setbacks as part of the journey, not signs of failure. When life gets tough, don't attach your worth to the outcome.*

You are worthy. You do have what it takes. **So why let life make you feel otherwise? How quickly can you bounce back after heartbreak, disappointment, or a setback?** Pain is temporary and doesn't last forever. Grace is your friend in hard moments. Learn from your past. Break harmful patterns. Find the lessons.

* *What did you learn from past situations?*
* *What can you do differently this time?*
* *Are you still holding onto a limiting belief about your past?*

Reflective learning brings confidence. Your past equips your resilience, wisdom, and perspective. Identify the skills you need to grow in grace and strength. Whenever I face challenges, I turn to God, the Most High. Divine wisdom brings clarity. Talking to God eases the heart and clears the mind.

There is a balance between hindsight, foresight, and insight. The same applies to the balance between your mind, body, and spirit. Working through uncomfortable moments with prayer, rest, or movement leads to mental clarity and peace. Romans 15:4 reminds us:

"For everything that was written in the past was written to teach us, so that through the endurance taught and the encouragement provided, we might have hope."

"Getting Your Feet Wet" is a mindset. It's through experience. It's about reflection, adaptability, grace, and resilience. The journey will be a process. Season by season. Brick by brick.

* *Are you ready for it?*

* *Do you want to follow the crowd or lead with purpose?*

* *Will you seek approval, or spark real change?*

Learn from you past to gain discernment. Celebrate the victories that came from every situation. Let the Holy Spirit guide your steps. Pray for clarity. Trust God with your future. Seek wisdom. Let your mind, body, and soul grow in harmony.

LOOK AT YOUR LIFE THROUGH HEAVENS EYES

4 In this chapter, we will explore life from a higher conscious perspective. Whether we admit it or not, we have all experienced moments of both heaven and hell during our time on earth. Experiencing heaven on earth is possible because life is filtered through the lens of our perception. Living life through Heaven's Eyes means viewing the world with compassion, hope, and a deeper sense of purpose. It means encouraging yourself to see beyond your circumstances and recognize the inherent value within yourself and others. In a world consumed by chaos, distractions, uncertainty, and strife. The chose to believe, *"God has plans greater than my*

current circumstance" can be transformative. A shift in perception changes not only our experiences, but how we engage with the world. When life is infused with compassion, hope, and purpose, every moment carries meaning.

When you decide to change how you see the world, you are no longer just participating in it. You begin to take ownership of your life and draw fulfillment from it. Compassion, hope, and purpose are the keys to this transformation.

Compassion

When you have compassion and empathy, it becomes easier to love others. Even those who are selfish, self-absorbed, or narcissistic. Compassion allows you to detach from someone else's reality and love them from a healthy distance. At the core of viewing life through Heaven's Eyes is compassion, and it is not simply a passive feeling.

It is a conscious decision to empathize with both the struggles and joys of others. This choice helps you remain emotionally grounded instead of reacting to words, or behaviors that could disturb your peace. Love never requires you to endure abuse, neglect, or malice. God would not call you to tolerate such things either. Loving beyond our own experiences allows you to recognize the larger tapestry of human existence.

Every person walking this earth carries burdens, dreams, and their own history. Acknowledging our shared humanity creates a connection that transcends superficial differences. Compassion helps us approach others with open hearts, kindness, and understanding, especially in a world where isolation is common. True compassion also works hand-in-hand with boundaries, which we will explore in another chapter.

Forgiveness & Hope

Hope begins with gratitude and forgiveness. Forgiveness releases resentment, anger, and bitterness, which only bind the heart to past pain. True forgiveness starts within. Forgive your decisions, your habits, the way you have treated yourself, and the lies you have believed. This kind of introspection requires strength, but within that strength lies freedom. Forgiveness heals old wounds, loosens the grip of the past, and opens doors to new possibilities. Choosing to view others with understanding does not mean you agree with them. It means you carry a sound mind and healed heart. Those who struggle with forgiveness often struggle with acceptance as well. Accountability is difficult, but without acknowledging your own flaws, true forgiveness will always feel out of reach. Without it, excuses easily become a crutch, allowing responsibility to be avoided.

Gratitude

The power of gratitude needs to remain a priority. In the rush of daily life, it is easy to overlook the simple blessings: the sounds of laughter, a quiet moment of stillness, the air in your lungs, and the warmth of the sun. These reminders bring you into the present moment, where God's presence can move freely in your life.

Gratitude is the foundation for all growth and transformation. It teaches us to appreciate every experience, even the hidden lessons within hardships. Gratitude shifts our focus from lack to abundance, reminding us that all blessings are temporary and meant to be cherished. Ask yourself:

❖ *What do I already have now that I haven't acknowledged?*

❖ *Do I recognize the gifts I have been given?*

❖ *Am I truly appreciating what I have been blessed with?*

❖ Across the world, many people cannot walk, touch, feel, see, or hear. Yet here you are, still able to experience life in ways others cannot. Surely you have something to be grateful for. Gratitude helps us recognize blessings even in hardship, giving us the ability to choose joy. This perspective fosters peace and contentment in the midst of life's complexities.

Purpose

Purpose is something many people spend their lives searching for. For some, life experiences reshape their sense of purpose, requiring reflection and reevaluation. Purpose is rarely revealed through a billboard declaring, "[Your

Name], *this is your purpose.*" More often, it is revealed through synchronicities, divine timing, and the guidance of the Most High, who places what you need directly in your path. Ironically, when we try to control everything, we block the very wisdom and direction we need. Many of us know the frustration of trying to force things our way, only to end up in a place of exhaustion.

Discovering your purpose requires preparation and alignment. When your purpose arrives, you want to recognize it and be ready to act. Cultivate the skills, habits, and mindset necessary to embrace what God has for you. Nothing is worse than missing an opportunity because you were not prepared. Align yourself with your vision, trust the process, and navigate life with resilience and faith. Hope fuels this pursuit. Hope keeps you moving forward when the path is unclear, reminding you that opportunities lie ahead. Many people lack hope simply because they do not understand its power to overcome fear.

- ❖ *Where should I being?*

- ❖ *Do I see how hope can cast fears away?*

- ❖ *What fears do I have that has been blocking the things I hope for?*

Authenticity & Alignment

My confidence comes from the Most High, and I stand firmly in who God called me to be. Ironically, the traits that make people uncomfortable are often the same ones they admire most. When you embrace authenticity, acknowledging both your strengths and weaknesses. You become resilient, vulnerable, teachable, optimistic, and capable of true leadership.

❖ *If you don't believe in yourself, who will?*

❖ *If you aren't honest with yourself, how can you expect others to believe you?*

❖ *If you lack compassion, gratitude, and love toward yourself, how can you expect the world to reflect that back to you?*

The truth is, you must embrace the fullness of who you were uniquely designed to be. Do not fall victim to the false narratives your mind may weave, convincing you otherwise. Self-deception only limits your growth. When you truly learn how to show up for yourself, you also learn how to show up for others.

Viewing life through Heaven's Eyes is an intentional choice. It is conscious commitment to live with compassion, gratitude, purpose, forgiveness, and hope. This higher perspective challenges us to rise above narrow thinking and embrace the interconnectedness we share. By cultivating these virtues, you enrich not only your own life but also the lives of everyone you encounter.

This transformation leads to a more meaningful and fulfilling existence, even in a world that often feels fragmented. Love, understanding, and purpose are always within your reach. God has already prepared a higher space for you. You are your own breakthrough. You are your own bridge.

RESPECTING YOUR LINE: IT'S OKAY TO PUT YOUR HAND UP

5 People will come into your life for various reasons: to hurt, to love, to heal, to leave, to take, to guide, to give, and more. Every person that crosses your path is meant to show you something. It could be how to treat yourself better, to forgive, to practice optimism, to love, or to stand up for yourself. Ultimately, everything in life is a lesson. In this chapter, the concept of "Putting Your Hand Up" revolves around your boundaries and not tolerating going outside of them. Boundaries are guidelines set to protect your personal space, well-being, and relationships. They establish healthy interactions: physical, emotional, mental, and relational. Maintaining healthy boundaries is

essential for self respect and to prevent burnout or resentment.

* *What are your boundaries?*

* *How do you pick yourself up when you fall?*

* *How do you communicate?*

* *Do you learn from your past experiences, or do you avoid them?*

* *Are you a taker or giver? Do people in your life give to you, or do they take from you?*

Boundaries & Self-Respect

It is important at times to revisit these questions regularly. One thing I truly appreciate is that boundaries are about taking actions for your own betterment. Setting boundaries doesn't mean treating others poorly or being unkind. To develop healthy boundaries, you must first know and accept who you are. Everyone has to define what they will or will not tolerate. Once you understand yourself, you can begin creating personal boundaries. For example, if you set a boundary not to eat after 7 p.m. but then break it, you weaken the commitment you made to yourself.

* *Do you know your triggers?*

* *Your weakness? Your strengths?*

* *Are you maintaining a balance in your emotional, mental, and physical well-being? How is your psychological state?*

* *If you're struggling to find balance, what steps are you taking to improve? Are you willing to keep working on it?*

Personal growth and setting the right atmosphere for yourself depend on how much effort you put into creating it intentionally. *"Treat others as you would yourself,"* a phrase we've heard before, holds true. If you respect yourself, you will respect others. If you love yourself, you will know how to love others. If you show up for yourself, you will be dependable for others. Personal boundaries help you define where your responsibilities end and where others' responsibilities begin. It ensures that you resist overextend yourself or allow others to take advantage of your niceness. Even with good intentions, everyone is different. This is why observation and communication are essential to understanding what others find appropriate and inappropriate. Boundaries will not look the same for everyone. Why? Because we all don't have the same values or code of conduct. Be mindful that your boundaries may not align with those around you, and that's okay. Avoid projecting expectations onto others if you aren't able to uphold them yourself. Too often, people create unrealistic demands because they refuse to look inward. Take time to reflect on your relationships with others and with yourself.

❖ *Have you taken the time to know the people in your life or are you projecting your own assumptions onto them?*

Grace, Balance, & Awareness

It's a natural instinct for people to project their insecurities, fears, needs, or desires. However, it's your responsibility to find your own respect and comfort in God. Finding comfort in God limits you from accepting others' fears onto yourself. A lack of boundaries can lead to mental and physical exhaustion. Give yourself grace, extend that same grace to others. You shouldn't fault people for the lack of knowledge, especially when it hasn't been effectively communicated. Instead, speak on things based on God's values and morals.

Guard Your Heart

"Above all else, guard your heart, for everything you do flows from it." Proverbs 4:23

Protecting Your Influence

"Do not be misled: 'Bad company corrupts good character.'" 1 Corinthians 15:33

Personal Space & Responsibility

"Make it your ambition to lead a quiet life: You should mind your own business and work with your hands, just as we told you, so that your daily life may win the respect of outsiders and so that you will not depend on anybody."

1 Thessalonians 4:11-12

Knowing Your Limits

"Seldom set foot in your neighbor's house—too much of you, and they will hate you." Proverbs 25:17

Anger & Personal Boundaries

"In your anger do not sin: Do not let the sun go down while you are still angry, and do not give the devil a foothold." Ephesians 4:26-27

A negative mindset needs to be recognized and cut at the root. It's equally important to feel comfortable with your 'no'. Negative thinking often leads to mental, emotional, spiritual, and physical consequences. Everyone experiences moments when their thoughts aren't aligned with positivity. The thoughts often arise from the darker parts of your consciousness mind, triggered by situations that stir them up. Awareness is where the real work begins. Any sadness, anger, fear, or disgust are emotions that need love and healing. Developing personal boundaries, even with yourself, is a vital part of this journey. You must learn to put your hand up to protect your well-being. This work will be hard, but it is profoundly beautiful. Believe in your ability to embrace the promises of your life, to live in a space of freedom and discipline. It's about balancing dualities without letting one overshadow the other.

Consequences of Living Without Boundaries

I want to express another concept that deals with people driven by bitterness, anguish, jealousy, envy, or judgement. Have sympathy for such individuals, because they often don't realize they're creating their own personal war zone in their minds. If you're unknowingly holding onto these traits, ask yourself: *How is this working for me? How is my body doing?* When you think, wish, or plan to intentionally harm others, it always comes with a price. You reap what you sow. Whatever ill you hope for someone else will eventually find its way back to you. Living with a good heart does not mean you are perfect. However, you can be perfectly imperfect, with a good heart, a kind soul, and a strong spirit. That, in itself, is a blessing from God, the Most High.

Generosity

"Remember this: Whoever sows sparingly will also reap sparingly, and whoever sows generously will also reap generously."
2 Corinthians 9:6

The Reward of the Wicked vs. the Righteous

"The wicked man earns deceptive wages, but he who sows righteousness reaps a sure reward."
Proverbs 11:18

<u>Giving and Receiving</u>

"Give, and it will be given to you. A good measure, pressed down, shaken together, and running over, will be poured into your lap. For with the measure you use, it will be measured to you."

Luke 6:38

Consequences of Evil

"As I have observed, those who plow evil and those who sow trouble reap it." Job 4:8

You are anointed, protected, and appointed, from above and below. Do you realize the power and favor that come with a pure heart? When you have favor from God, especially while protecting yourself, your loved ones, or your community, you are blessed with strength for battle. Faith without works is dead. You can wish and pray, but without action behind your words, your efforts are wasted.

Setting boundaries does not mean stonewalling, gaslighting, or manipulating to gain control. Those are low-vibrational tactics. Give yourself time and space to reflect, reconnect, and find peace when you feel like you have none. Be 100% honest with others about your boundaries and non-negotiable, especially regarding respect.

Respect is something many of us should have been taught as children. In today's world, we see children who don't know respect and only know fear. Parents are meant to teach, demonstrate, and enforce respect with love. When children grow up responding out of fear rather than respect, it creates a generational problem.

All parents do not use fear to gain respect. Many use love to earn it and I am grateful for that. However, if this topic makes you uncomfortable, ask yourself why. *Why does invoking fear in others feel uncomfortable to acknowledge?* Every parent should aim to lead their children to God and gain respect through love and personal boundaries. When you encounter people who use fear and power to control, it often reveals that they themselves are fearful. To truly assist others, allow them to reflect and express vulnerability. There are many ways to uproot anything that holds a person back, but it must start with love and prayer.

If you find yourself unhappy with how people are treating you, ask yourself why you are allowing it. If you're going into work every weekday and being treated poorly, *why are you choosing to stay in a place where you aren't appreciated?* The same applies to friendships, family, and relationships. I'm not saying to leave just because you're upset or passive. Making decisions purely from emotions is unwise and demonstrates a lack of control. However, whatever you do not learn or address in your current season, will follow you. It will show up in different faces, places, or circumstances until you learn to establish boundaries for your healing and mind. What you choose to indulge in becomes your reality. Free will is the gift God has given, but be prepared to lie in the bed you make.

HOW OFTEN DO YOU TAKE A STEP BACK

6 When was the last time you stepped back, not just to observe the world around you, but to truly observe yourself?

* *To watch your thoughts, your actions, your life?*

* *To reflect on the seeds you've planted or the ones you've neglected to water over the years?*

* *How do you rationalize your mind?*

Taking a step back means creating space for reflection and allowing introspection. It doesn't mean getting lost in your thoughts. Rather, it's about taking intentional, temporary breaks. Once a day, once a week, or whenever your schedule allows. Use this time to reflect deeply. We often desire, crave, and hope for things without dedicating time to understanding ourselves. This is not about brainstorming your next big idea, solving a problem, or strategizing how to turn your vision into reality. It's about becoming the kind of person who can sustain the vision you're working toward. Many people pray to God, asking or demanding what they want. *If it was that simple, wouldn't we all already have everything we desire?* The key lies in aligning yourself with the frequency of what you wish to attract. While many talk about this concept, few live by it. Yet, some embody it unknowingly, which is a beauty in disguise. Personal growth requires commitment and consistency. It involves evolving daily, expanding your mind, enhancing your energy, and reshaping your life to match your deepest desires. Life is a marathon of introspection, not a sprint. Along the way, you will learn lessons about love, patience, willingness, persistence, and discipline. You will come to understand that nothing in life is easy, but constant transformative. Those who choose this path will find joy in the process. They learn to appreciate both the success and self-discovery it brings. You will be amazed at how much you're truly capable of achieving.

There has been many moments in my life when I needed to pause and reflect, even in the midst of chaos. While my life has often been peaceful, I've always been an empathetic person, deeply attuned to the experiences of others. It's a gift from God, allowing me to learn and grow through others without being burned by the fire. During these moments of reflection even in the presence of negativity, I've found clarity. I've been able to see, understand, and relate to others while remaining present. These reflections have reminded me of an essential truth: you gain the ability to see beyond yourself. For many, stepping outside their own perspective is a struggle. It's even more challenging for some, not to take things personally. These difficulties can make honest conversations and meaningful dialogue feel nearly impossible. There's an old saying: "*If the shoes fits, wear it.*" This phrase passed down through generations, offers a simple reminder of self-awareness and humility. It encourages us to reflect on whether criticism or feedback applies to us. If so, accept it with grace.

When you take moments to step outside of yourself, even while caught up in your own situation or thoughts. You gain a unique perspective. You begin to observe your thinking patterns and uncover the reasons behind them. This practice turns you into your own best student, allowing you to learn from your own mind. This is the first step toward self-discovery: becoming an observer of your own life. *Do you take the time to observe your thoughts, your self-talk, and how you evaluate situations?* When you embrace the role of being both your greatest teacher and your greatest lesson, you begin the process of mastering yourself. You develop a deeper understanding of your strengths, weaknesses, habits, and thought pattens.

❖ *Have you ever stopped to consider the environment within your own mind?*

❖ *What kind of mindset do you want to cultivate?*

❖ *Is your mindset driven by negativity such as harsh self-talk, judgement of others, or pessimistic thinking? If so, ask yourself why you continue to participate in that narrative.*

When you ignore the environment of your mind, you risk staying stuck in denial. You remain captive to the same patterns you continue to feed. Anxiety, fear, depression, and anger often arise from how you interpret your experiences; how you speak to yourself. Those emotions do not control you. You have the power and the authority. You are not weak, fearful, clueless, or broken. Many of you are far stronger than you give yourselves credit for. You can attend workshops, seminars and personal development events. However, if you don't apply what you've learned and begin observing of your thoughts. You'll never truly understand the role you play in shaping your own life. If you want to attract better things, it all begins with the environment you cultivate in your mind.

CROSS BETWEEN TWO ROADS

7 *"Trust in the Lord with all your heart and lean not on your own understanding; in all your ways submit to Him, and He will make your paths straight." Proverbs 3:5-6*

For I know the plans I have for you," declares the Lord, "plans to prosper you and not to harm you, plans to give you a hope and a future." Jeremiah 29:11

Everyone faces decisions of whether to go left or right, what is right or wrong. *Should you move to a new city? Should you start your own business?* So many "ifs," so many worries, and unnecessary anxiety. It's the constant battle between the mind and our gut.

* *Why do we feel in our gut that something is good, yet allow our minds to convince us otherwise?*

* *Why do we sense in our gut that something is "bad" and our minds convince us that it is okay? What is healthy or unhealthy for you at this moment?*

Many of us grapple with relationships, careers, or even simple everyday decisions. We can find ourselves going back and forth, battling between the gut and the mind. No journey will lead you to the right path as effectively as following your gut. Your gut is the centerpiece of your spiritual essence. It's connected to the divine guidance of God within your soul to steer your steps in this world. Based on your life experiences, you may not have trusted your gut. As a result, you might not be accustomed to listening to it. The gut is like a muscle. The more you train it, the more you will feel it, hear it, and act on it.

We all have challenges of worry, overthinking, procrastinating, excuses, impulses, and more. *However, when do you take the time to sit and truly listen to your intuition?* Everyone will be guided towards the journey they are meant to take. This is why freeing yourself from overthinking removes the confusion and creates peace in the presence of God. Uncertainty is often an underestimated part of everyone's life. It leaves you wondering what will happen and what you should do. I've had many "ah-ha" moments when reflecting on the mysteries of life. Everything has a pattern, a heartbeat, and within that lies uncertainty.

Trusting God is crucial when making decisions in your life. Equally important is learning to trust yourself. *How many times have you placed all your faith in something or someone else, yet denied yourself that same trust?* Trusting yourself is something that is learned. Even children have to learn to trust, and they often act on impulses. However, as an adult navigating the complexities of life, impulsive reactions can lead to significant consequences. Acting without thought can cost you what matters the most, when you don't take time to assess.

It's crucial to take the time to assess every situation and trust your instincts when making decisions. This process is like training a muscle, developing and strengthening your intuition over time. As you learn to listen to your gut, you improve your ability to make the best decisions for yourself. It's important not blame yourself for past mistakes. You made the best decision you could with the information you had at the time. Trusting your gut is also an act of faith, as it aligns with trusting in God. God provides an immense sense of peace when we listen to the obedience within our hearts. However, the mind can often play tricks on us. It can create illusions or resurrect past scenarios, making you feel as though those situations are happening again. *Have you ever experienced a new change in your life, only to have negative patterns from the past resurface?* Your mind can even make you believe something happened when it never actually took place. Recognizing these mental patterns helps you stay grounded in truth and trust in divine guidance for the healing you need.

When you're stuck at a crossroads, Psalm 37:4 reminds us that when your desires align with God, your intuition may reflect the desires by the seeds being planted in your heart. When your heart is tuned to its purpose, you're naturally in sync with God's will. During these moments, your ego may try to take over. The ego often seeks to validate emotions through our thoughts, which can lead to even greater conflict and confusion. There is a difference between ego and confidence. Ego thrives on external validation and pride. Confidence comes from a deep grounded understanding of yourself. Therefore, any decision you make, let it be from confidence. Let it stem from the quiet assurance of knowing who you are and trusting God to guide your steps in every step of the way.

The constant pull between the gut and mind can feel like an endless battle.

* *Do you place more faith in your own abilities and knowledge than in the source of all pure intelligence?*

* *Are you caught in the mental tug-of-war between what is right and what is wrong?*

* *Does your mind have more control over you than your intuition?*

* *How did it turn out for you when you listened to your mind? How did they unfold when you followed your intuition? Do you see the difference when you reflect?*

At the core, it's about what is healthy for you. Make decisions and guide your thoughts in a way that aligns with the divine path set for you. When you choose not to trust God and rely solely on your own understanding, you remove God from the equation. When you remove God from the equation, you remove yourself. This disconnection leads to confusion, doubt, worry, and disbelief. Many people confuse intuition with familiarity, patterns from past experiences or interactions with others. Your intuition is not rooted in past experiences. Surrender it all. Surrender to God to set yourself free and gain the provision you need. Surrendering is an act that we choose to take, to gain the insight and peace we need. If you are obsessively steadfast, it causes you mental stress. You are unknowingly making the person, place, or thing an idol. When you choose to surrender yourself to allow God to be the priority, you will not be in a battle with the body and mind.

You cannot move forward with confidence by being in a "in-between" state, whether it's in relationships, business, or life decisions. God will make the unseen visible and the unclear unmistakably clear. You will receive clarity not only about situations but also about your perception of others. When you feel like you are battling internally; pause. The unanswered will become clear, along with divine guidance on the direction you should take. Your mind may play tricks and your emotions can mislead you. When you step into your authority within your spirit, everything will subside.

WHAT ARE YOU WILLING TO SACRIFICE TO BECOME YOUR GREATER SELF?

8

"But he gives us more grace. That is why Scripture says: 'God opposes the proud but shows favor to the humble.'"

- James 4:6

"The greatest among you will be your servant. For those who exalt themselves will be humbled, and those who humble themselves will be exalted." - Matthew 23:11-12

What is next for your spiritual, physical, mental, and physiological ascension? As you navigate life, be mindful of what you indulge your heart and time in. Don't allow your current journey to lead to complacency. Instead, cultivate a spirit that seeks to always be content in God. Consider with gratitude life's challenges and rewards; facing them with humility. Keep your heart open so you can resist anger, be quick to listen, and eager to understand. You'll discover more about yourself and learn how to heal in every aspect where you feel a void. The key to receiving everything you desire in life lies in authenticity and growth in a place of light. Embrace your true essence in alignment with God.

The majority of enlightenment from my experiences has come naturally through spending time alone, traveling the world, enjoying my own company, respecting differing opinions, and listening to the wise words of others who displayed fruit. Many experiences that occurs within self-discovery require you to make sacrifices of your old ways to evolve into your higher appointed self. I want to encourage you to find meaningful activities for yourself that go beyond what is worldly appealing, until you develop personal discipline.

The key to receiving everything you desire in life lies in authenticity and growth. Your life experiences is your playground for gaining wisdom. Open your mind to diverse perceptions; understand how people think, feel, and place yourself in their shoes. You will learn from the life experiences of others, giving you valuable insight to ponder on. *Have you noticed how children raised by older generations often grew up to be wise, intelligent, and observant?* Compare this to children raised by adults who aren't "awakened" to implant good values within them. It is like night and day.

The beauty is, the learning process doesn't stop when we become adults. Many adults in today's world struggle with ability to observe, think critically, form conclusions rooted in reality and truth. If you've been told that you are difficult to communicate with, or one-sided in your thinking; it doesn't mean you are unintelligent. It might mean you're unwise due to resisting growth and clinging to limited beliefs based solely on your perceptions. A new city, a new place or a new experience to transform your perception. Ask yourself if your thoughts, beliefs, and actions align with God's will for your life.

Many people want so much from life but lack the inner drive to achieve their goals. Relying on external sources to make things happen is wishful and falsified thinking. Manipulation, deception, and falsehoods will lead to personal downfall until you take ownership of yourself.

I share my thoughts and wisdom God gave to me because I want everyone to realize their potential and be amazed by what you can achieve when they commit to doing the inner work. While you don't have to go through the journey alone, in beginning it may seem like you are alone. Only you can shift yourself into an aligned mindset. If things aren't working in your favor or as you hoped; take a moment to pay attention. Sometimes, falling and failing are necessary to learn the lessons life is trying to teach you. *What is the lesson?* You can't afford to get lost in dreams and manifestations without putting in the effort to grow spiritually and mentally. As you encounter different seasons in life, use them as periods of reflection. When something doesn't go as expected, ask yourself:

❖ *What am I missing? What do I need to focus on to align myself with what is meant for me?*

When you seek with intentions, you find the answers. When you find alignment within yourself, you will attract everything that resonate with it. God has placed everyone here for a unique purpose, even when that purpose may not seem clear. Take it one step at a time. Put one foot in front of the other, until your vision becomes clear. If you already have clarity, focus on doing what you can and should, then leave the rest to God. Remember, you must be willing to sacrifice who you are, for who you will become.

"The most difficult thing is the decision to act, the rest is merely tenacity." -Amelia Earhart

" *The more you are motivated by love, the more fearless and free your action will be.*" - Dalai Lama

"*You have to give up the life you planned in order to have the life that is waiting for you.*" - Joseph Campbell

"*If you want something you've never had, you must be willing to do something you've never done.*" - Thomas Jefferson

www.ingramcontent.com/pod-product-compliance
Lightning Source LLC
Chambersburg PA
CBHW071110090426
42737CB00013B/2559